A Picture Book of
Jackie Robinson

David A. Adler

illustrated by Robert Casilla

Holiday House/New York

To my nephew, Hillel David Neumark
D.A.A.
To the memory of my beloved Uncle Ben
R.C.

Library of Congress Cataloging-in-Publication Data
Adler, David A.
A picture book of Jackie Robinson / David A. Adler ; illustrated
by Robert Casilla.—1st ed.
p.   cm.
ISBN 0-8234-1122-2
1. Robinson, Jackie, 1919-1972—Juvenile literature. 2. Baseball
players—United States—Biography—Juvenile literature.
[1. Robinson, Jackie, 1919-1972. 2. Baseball players. 3. Afro-
Americans—Biography.]   I. Casilla, Robert, ill.   II. Title.
GV865.R6A646   1994   93-27224   CIP   AC
796.357'092—dc20
[B]

Other books in David A. Adler's *Picture Book Biography* series

A Picture Book of George Washington

A Picture Book of Abraham Lincoln

A Picture Book of Martin Luther King, Jr.

A Picture Book of Thomas Jefferson

A Picture Book of Benjamin Franklin

A Picture Book of Helen Keller

A Picture Book of Eleanor Roosevelt

A Picture Book of Christopher Columbus

A Picture Book of John F. Kennedy

A Picture Book of Simón Bolívar

A Picture Book of Harriet Tubman

A Picture Book of Florence Nightingale

A Picture Book of Jesse Owens

A Picture Book of Anne Frank

A Picture Book of Frederick Douglass

A Picture Book of Sitting Bull

A Picture Book of Rosa Parks

A Picture Book of Robert E. Lee

A Picture Book of Sojourner Truth

Jack Roosevelt Robinson was born on January 31, 1919, in a small, old farmhouse near Cairo, Georgia. His parents were Mallie and Jerry Robinson. Jackie's grandfather had been a slave. Jackie was the youngest of five children.

His father worked on Jim Sasser's plantation, but he worked for such low wages that his wife said, "We're no better off than slaves."

Jerry Robinson complained to the owner of the plantation. After that he was no longer paid wages. Instead he became a sharecropper. He kept a share of whatever he grew and gave the rest to Sasser.

In July 1919, Jerry Robinson said he was leaving to look for better work. He traveled by train to Florida and didn't come back.

After Jerry Robinson left, Sasser told Mallie and her children to leave, too. Mallie worked as a maid for a while. Then, in May 1920, she took her family west to Pasadena, California, where her brother Burton lived. He had urged her to join him, and "get a little closer to heaven."

For an African-American family, Pasadena was not quite heaven. The public pool was open only one day a week to blacks. In the movie theaters, blacks had to sit separately from whites, in the balcony.

On Pepper Street, where the Robinsons lived, one neighbor called the police because his wife was afraid of African-Americans. The white neighbors cursed the Robinsons and even threw rocks at them. They tried to scare them out and then to buy them out. But Mallie wouldn't move.

Jackie loved games and sports. He played dodgeball, stickball, jacks, and marbles. He played to win and usually did.

At John Muir Technical High School and Pasadena Junior College, Jackie Robinson starred in track and field, football, basketball, and baseball. At the University of California at Los Angeles (UCLA) he was a football hero and the first student to star in four sports.

In 1940, at UCLA, Jackie Robinson met Rachel Isum, a smart, beautiful nursing student.

At first Rachel didn't like Jackie. She thought he was arrogant. But they talked, and she realized she was wrong. Jackie was a warm and sensitive man.

Jackie Robinson left UCLA in the spring of 1941, a short time before he would have graduated. He wanted to work and earn money to help his mother.

Jackie went to Hawaii, where he joined the Honolulu Bears, a professional football team willing to have an African-American play for them.

On December 7, 1941, the Japanese bombed Pearl Harbor, Hawaii, near where Jackie had lived. Luckily he was already on a ship heading back to California. Following the attack the United States entered the Second World War. In 1942, Jackie Robinson was drafted into the army and sent to Fort Riley, Kansas.

Jackie complained when he was kept off the army baseball team because he was black. He complained, too, that the camp post exchange (PX) restaurant had separate sections for black and white soldiers.

Jackie Robinson and other African-Americans at Fort Riley applied for training to be officers. They were turned down because they were black.

Jackie spoke to Joe Louis, an African-American, the heavyweight boxing champion of the world and, for a while, a soldier at Fort Riley. A few days later Jackie and other African-Americans were admitted to officer candidate school.

The army sent Lieutenant Robinson to Camp Hood, Texas. There on a bus the driver told him, "Get to the back where colored people belong."

Separate seating on an army bus was no longer allowed. Jackie Robinson didn't move. At the last stop, the military police took him to their duty officer. They argued, and in August 1944, Robinson was court-martialed—put on trial by the army—for not showing respect to the officer. Jackie Robinson was judged to be innocent, but he had had enough of army life. He was released a few months later.

In 1945, professional baseball was a segregated sport. There were no African-Americans playing on any of the major-league teams. They played in the Negro Leagues on teams such as the Homestead Grays, the Birmingham Black Barons, and the Kansas City Monarchs. After Jackie

Robinson left the army, he played shortstop for the Monarchs. He was a good fielder and hitter and a fast, smart base runner.

Negro Leagues baseball attracted large crowds, sometimes even larger than all-white major-league teams playing in the same city.

Jackie Robinson didn't know it, but among the thousands of people who watched him play were scouts for the Brooklyn Dodgers. Branch Rickey, the president of the all-white team, had decided it was time that major-league baseball become a truly national game open to all players, black and white.

The scouts were looking for an African-American player who was good enough to help the team win and brave enough to be the first black in the all-white major leagues.

On August 28, 1945, Branch Rickey met Jackie Robinson. Rickey told Robinson that he'd like him to play for the Dodgers, but he could expect trouble. Rickey said, "I'm looking for a ballplayer with guts enough not to fight back."

In 1946, Jackie Robinson played for the Montreal Royals, the Dodgers' top minor-league team. That year, he also married Rachel Isum, the beautiful nursing student he had met at U.C.L.A. They had three children, Jack Jr., Sharon, and David.

In April 1947, Jackie Robinson reported to the Brooklyn Dodgers.

At first, in some cities, he could not stay in the same hotels as his white teammates nor eat in the same restaurants. Ballplayers on other teams threatened to strike, and not play the Dodgers. They insulted Robinson and even kicked him. He received letters threatening him and his family.

Baseball players and fans said that the "Robinson experiment" wouldn't work and that blacks and whites couldn't play on the same baseball team. Jackie Robinson proved they were wrong.

The year 1947, Robinson's first on the Dodgers, was said to be "the toughest first season any ballplayer has faced." At the end of it, Robinson was selected Rookie of the Year, for being the best first-year player in the major leagues. In 1949, he was selected as the Most Valuable Player in the National League.

While Jackie Robinson played for the Dodgers, the team won six National League pennants, and each time they played the New York Yankees in the World Series. The Dodgers won in 1955 and were major-league baseball's world champions.

JACK ROOSEVELT ROBINSON

BROOKLYN N.L. 1947 TO 1956
LEADING N.L. BATTER

Until after the 1956 season, when Robinson retired, he was one of the best players in baseball. In 1962, he was the first African-American inducted into baseball's Hall of Fame.

In 1956, Jackie Robinson was awarded the Spingarn Medal for his sportsmanship and his work with young African-Americans.

In the years following his retirement from baseball, Robinson worked as a vice president of Chock Full o'Nuts restaurants. He was active in the efforts to get equal rights for African-Americans, and he helped established the Freedom National Bank in Harlem, New York City.

Jackie Robinson was stricken with diabetes and heart disease. He died of a heart attack on October 24, 1972. He was just fifty-three years old.

Jackie Robinson was a gifted athlete, but it was his courage more than his ability to play baseball that made him truly great. Being the first African-American player in major-league baseball was an important step toward equal rights for all Americans.

AUTHOR'S NOTE

In 1872, Bud Fowler became the very first African-American to play professional baseball on a team with whites. There were others, but by 1892, outside of the Negro Leagues, professional baseball was for whites only.

The Dodgers are in major-league baseball's National League. In July 1947, Larry Doby joined the Cleveland Indians and became the first African-American in the American League.

Monte Irvin, an African-American who followed Robinson to the big leagues, said that Jackie Robinson "opened the door of baseball to all men." Elston Howard, the first African-American to play for the New York Yankees said, "He meant everything to a black ballplayer. . . . He did it for all of us."

IMPORTANT DATES

1919	Born on January 31 near Cairo, Georgia.
1920	Moved to Pasadena, California, in May.
1939–1941	Starred on football, baseball, basketball, and track teams at UCLA.
1942–1944	Served in the U.S. Army.
1945	Played professional baseball on the Kansas City Monarchs of the Negro Leagues.
1945	Met Branch Rickey on August 28. Signed baseball contract with Dodgers on October 23.
1946	Played for the Montreal Royals.
1946	Married Rachel Isum on February 10.
1947–1956	Played professional baseball for the Brooklyn Dodgers.
1947	Named National League Rookie of the Year.
1949	Named National League Most Valuable Player.
1956	Awarded the Spingarn Medal.
1957	Announced retirement from baseball on January 5 and began work for Chock Full o'Nuts.
1962	Elected to baseball Hall of Fame.
1972	Died on October 24 in Stamford, Connecticut.